Although every one of us wants to let go and experience the pleasure of our sexuality, it is not as simple as it seems. For until we are able to accept our fears and our shames without judgment, we are not free to experience sexual pleasure fully. Each of us has deeply implanted ideas about sexuality and how we should behave sexually.

This unique book will help you move toward a heightened sexual awareness and experience the joy and celebration of sex.

THE THOUGHT-A-WEEK GUIDES: HOW TO HAVE A BETTER SEX LIFE

A Blue Cliff
Editions Book

Barbara Glabman-Cohen

BALLANTINE BOOKS • NEW YORK

Library of Congress Catalog Card Number: 86-91651

ISBN 0-345-33343-8

Manufactured in the United States of America

First Edition: May 1987

To my mother and father,
whose love was an inspiration.

ACKNOWLEDGEMENTS

To Meridith, Jimmy, and Leslie, who asked me so many questions about this wonderful subject, SEX, and to my dear husband, William, who helped me, supported me, and listened to me while I was giving birth to this book. Each has taught me about the joy of sex in his or her own way. And a special thanks to Arlene Harris Shulman, without whom this book couldn't have been written.

CONTENTS

1. Childhood memories about sex affect me as an adult. 3
2. I know how I feel about pornography. 7
3. I understand the sounds of love. 11
4. Sex and love can mean two different things. 13
5. My entire being is my sexual instrument. 15
6. Fear is the opposite of love. 17
7. If I were a man/If I were a woman ... 19
8. Sex is fun. 21
9. I will have no more "shoulds." 23
10. I know how to speak sexually. 25
11. I deserve to receive love. 27
12. I have the right to say no. 29
13. Ladies and Gentlemen—introducing your genitals. 31
14. I can feel good about pleasuring myself. 35
15. I free myself from ideas of normal and planned sexuality. 37

16. I know and appreciate my body.   39
17. I know what excites me and turns me on.   41
18. Foreplay is the doorway to pleasure.   43
19. Freeing my pelvis leads to greater sexual
    pleasure.   45
20. Vibrators can be liberating.   49
21. What to do if I'm just not turned on.   53
22. My sexual fantasies are a banquet.   55
23. My partner and I take turns "going first."   59
24. I understand the human sexual response
    cycle.   61
25. I can relax and let go.   63
26. Touching me, touching you.   67
27. Withheld anger decreases sexual enjoyment.   69
28. I create a good atmosphere for lovemaking.   73
29. I will do the things I've never done before.   75
30. I set aside enough time for sexual pleasure.   77
31. Deep breathing enhances sexual pleasure.   79
32. Massage can be a doorway to a heightened
    sexual experience.   81
33. Orgasm can be a peak experience for me.   83
34. I luxuriate in the afterglow of sex.   85
35. There are many ways to reach orgasm.   87
36. There's more to sex than orgasm.   89
37. Letting go of false myths about orgasm may
    being me greater pleasure.   91
38. I choose to follow my positive sexual
    teachings.   95
39. I don't take my mind to bed.   99
40. Mutual trust allows for greater surrender.   101
41. The greatest lover is the person who loves
    himself.   103
42. Giving to my lover is giving to me.   105
43. I can have kinky sex without guilt.   107
44. Cleanliness can enhance sexual pleasure.   109
45. Sex can be a dance.   111

46. Water meditation can increase sexual pleasure. 113
47. I ask for what I like and say what I don't like. 115
48. Keeping the excitement in my long-term relationship. 117
49. I will not follow habits that limit my sexuality. 119
50. I reclaim my sexual innocence. 121
51. Taking precautions takes the worry out of sex. 123
52. Saying yes to sex. 125
53. I accept the ups and downs of my sexual life. 127

INTRODUCTION

"The profound importance of sex lies in the intense pleasure it offers human beings. Pleasure for human beings
is not a luxury, but a profound psychological need."
                                        —Nathaniel Branden

We all say we want pleasure. Yet sex has become a very
serious business. For many, this striving for sexual pleasure
has made the sexual union a battle, an obligation, or a
performance that is indeed barren of pleasure. Sex has become the focus of survival for the many who know no other
form of love.

Our sexuality reflects the totality of our being. It is an
expression of what we value, and of all our beliefs. How
we behave in bed is a mirror of who we are.

Although every one of us wants to let go and experience
the pleasure of our sexuality, it is not as simple as it seems.
For until we are able to accept our fears and our shames
without judgment, we are not free to experience sexual

1

pleasure fully. Each of us has been programmed with deeply implanted ideas about sexuality and how we should behave sexually. For this reason, we often have conditioned responses to images and events in our environment, rather than responding to these stimuli with our spontaneous feelings.

The seed thoughts offered here will help you move toward a heightened sexual awareness. They will show you how to explore gently your own sexual thoughts and preconceptions. Indeed, when you are able to let go of your body, rather than listening to the shoulds of your past and the demands of the future, you can allow yourself to respond to your own excitement and pleasure.

As you read this book, keep this thought in mind: Sex is not a duty, or an obligation, but an expression of joy, a gift, and a celebration of who you are.

Childhood memories about sex affect me as an adult.

☐

For each of us, childhood memories about sex affect our sexual behavior today. For some, these memories are gentle and loving and have helped us to become warm, sensual adults. For many of us, the memories are troublesome, filling us with shame and making us think that sex is dirty. This may have led us to be fearful and distrustful of sexual relationships. This week, we will explore some of the experiences that have molded our sexual history, examine how they have formed our attitudes, and try to change the areas that cause us problems.

It is not easy to move back into the past and reconstruct your history. Appreciate your willingness to explore such a sensitive area. Your willingness to embark on this adventure will bring you new insights and will be extremely helpful in creating a healthier, freer sexual identity.

Here is a list of questions to begin with. When you ask yourself these questions, take all the time you need to allow images of the past to materialize. Notice the feelings that surround these memories. Take notes to record these thoughts: they'll give you an idea of what the child in you thinks and feels about sex. This can lead you to better understand your sexual self.

- What childhood memories do you have about your body?
- Do you remember examining your body?
- Were you allowed to walk around naked?
- Was there nudity in your home?
- What were the parts of your body called?
- When and how did you discover that you were a boy or a girl?
- Did you have an early sexual experience with another child?
- Did you have an early sexual experience with an adult?
- What was it like?
- What messages did you receive from your parents about sexual exploration?
- When did you first see another naked body? What were your feelings?
- Did you masturbate? How did you feel when you did?

After you have asked yourself these questions, you will be able to complete this sentence:

The child in me believes that sex is

_____.

The next step is to let go of those childhood beliefs and educate your inner child. Introduce a new way of looking at yourself. First, tell the child in you that life is not what it was then. Be reassured that sex is pleasurable and it is now okay to enjoy it. Be gentle as you engage in this reeducation. The child in you will need your clarity, your compassion, and your wisdom to mature. It may take time, but the inner freedom that you gain will be worth the effort.

I know how I feel about pornography.

The dictionary defines pornography as "written or pictorial matter intended to arouse sexual feelings." Today there is an increasing number of sexually explicit materials on the market. There are books, magazines, videotapes, and movies that leave nothing to the imagination. In relation to the Supreme Court's 1974 decision on pornography, Justice Potter Stewart, who had been among those asked to review the film *Carnal Knowledge,* said that he could not define pornography, but he would know it when he saw it. This line of reasoning puts the responsibility for pornography with you—in the viewer's hands.

This week, allow yourself to use Justice Stewart's stance as a guideline for exploring your own beliefs about pornography. It will give you an opportunity to better understand your thoughts and feelings and perhaps allow you to stretch their limits.

The first part of the exercise is to complete these sentences:

- I have never seen any sexually explicit material. Yes ___ No ___
- If I have, it made me feel _____.
- When I see a male/female body engaged in the sex act, I feel _____.
- These magazines and books reveal _____.

The second step is to go to a newsstand and spend some time looking at the sex magazines. Note what you are feeling. Are your hands sweaty? Does your face feel red? Notice what is happening in your body. What messages are you giving yourself? Are you concerned with what the other people are thinking? If you can, allow yourself to purchase a magazine. See how many magazines are for sale, and realize how many people are also purchasing these magazines.

Now when you are at home, go through the magazine. Is there anything that turns you on? Is there anything that you like or dislike? Can you accept that pornography may be helpful at times, by illustrating different sexual techniques? Or by helping you know that others have the same fantasies that you might have judged yourself for or felt guilty about? Or does it make you feel that sex is "dirty," mechanical, or distorted? Allow yourself to explore what you think.

The idea here is that you can make a choice, and that as a consenting adult, it is your right to choose what feels good for you. Exploring what you believe about pornography is taking another step toward accepting who you are sexually. If you enjoy it and find it helpful, don't hesitate to use it. If it disturbs you or makes you uncomfortable, don't bother with it. The important thing is to make a personal choice and allow others the same freedom, even though it may differ from yours.

I understand the
sounds of love.

Are you aware that many people make love silently? Not only do they withhold their likes and dislikes, but they do not allow themselves to "talk dirty," or even to make sounds of appreciation. Do you fall into this category? If so, it's time to explore the sounds of sex.

Making love is a total expression of who you are. For many, "talking dirty" is one way of adding spice to making love. In that special moment, they are choosing to leave the good little girl or boy at home. They are playing out a fantasy, and they are "hot." Do you know that most people get turned on by hearing that their partner is excited, too? Adding words is adding another ingredient to the experience.

Sounds add the harmony to an already exciting beat. Moans and wails can heighten your arousal. Let your motor purr; allow your laughter to roar; do not hold back the sounds of your love and joy. Do not stifle your expressions of excitement. Expressing who you are, your enjoyment, your pleasure, will add to the experience and also turn your partner on.

On the physical level, letting out sounds during love-making seems to increase the level of excitement—sounds can carry you to new heights of stimulation. At the moment of orgasm, a scream or moan can facilitate the release of all the sexual energy that has been building up and help you to land fully satisfied in a delicious afterglow.

This week, when you make love, experiment with sounds. If this is new to you, start gently. First, allow yourself to breathe heavily. Then increase these sounds to moans. If you are feeling daring, let out a few yells. It may take practice and getting used to the sound of your own voice. It may also take some courage to risk such explosions in front of your partner. But the results should be worth it. So close the windows and doors and forget about what the neighbors will think.

Sex and love can mean two different things.

☐

Many of us often confuse love and lust and end up disguising our need for pure physical sexual enjoyment as a need for love. Because of this, we get involved in relationships for the wrong reasons. We may tell ourselves we want to be seriously involved with someone and even lead our partner to think we want to make a commitment, when what we are really looking for is a sexual adventure, with no strings attached. A similar problem arises for someone who so wants to get involved that he will attach himself to anyone he can, always thinking he has found his true love —when what he's really found is an enjoyable evening of sexual pleasure, no more, no less.

Neither of these types of people is facing his feelings about sex and love. They can't admit their sexual desires or need for love to themselves, so they can't convey them to anyone else. This week, we will explore what you think about the link between sex and love.

Whatever you come to accept about sex and love, it is

important for you to be honest with yourself. That is the only way you will be able to share yourself fully with others and to experience the satisfaction you are seeking.

Begin by asking yourself whether you are comfortable having sex without love or commitment. It is a very individual issue. Just because your friends have casual sex doesn't mean it is right for you. In fact, if it is not for you and you continue having sexual encounters of this nature, it may have a negative influence on your self-respect and can eventually affect your ability to enjoy sex.

Now ask yourself whether you may be denying yourself some very enjoyable moments if you say no to sex because you hold to a rigid belief that love and sex must go together. It is possible to have a pleasurable and exciting sexual encounter without love—as long as you know what you are getting into.

This week, find out where you stand on the issue of sex and love. It's up to you to discover what is right for you. Then have the bravery to stick to your beliefs. Whatever you decide, your honesty with yourself will have a positive effect on your sex life.

My entire being is my sexual instrument.

☐

When people talk about their sexual instrument, they are usually referring to their penis or vagina—and more often than not, their reference is either boastful or self-deprecating. This "locker-room" emphasis on genitalia is one thing that can distort our sexual outlook. This week, consider every inch of your body, from the top of your head to the tip of your toes, as your sexual instrument. Keep in mind that every inch of your skin has the potential for giving you pleasure. One of the most important aspects of having pleasure in the sexual experience is knowing what pleases you and taking the responsibility of asking for that pleasure.

This exercise is an opportunity for you to tune in to your body and to get to know what brings you pleasure. Take the next half hour just for yourself. Unplug the phone. Find a comfortable place to lie down. Now, just let go of your mind. This is your time to explore.

Now that you are lying down, close your eyes and turn

your attention to your breathing. Create a natural rhythm
. . . breathing in, and breathing out . . . just relaxing with
each new breath.

Begin to allow your hands to explore every inch of your
body—as if you were a child discovering your body for
the first time. Use your hands creatively . . . exploring,
poking, and massaging . . . using different strokes to explore what feels good. Be aware of the textures of the different parts of your body. Feel the temperature changes. If
you are uncomfortable about touching yourself, just allow
this feeling to register. Discover what arouses you sexually
and what feels good sensually. As you continue this personal exploration, be aware of your attitudes—but don't
judge your thoughts or feelings. It's all right if negative
feelings come up—they are also a part of your total sexual
awareness. Just feeling them is an accomplishment, too.

When you have completed your exploration, breathe
deeply. Enjoy the quiet. Now stretch and finish this sentence:

Right now my body feels
_____.

Fear is the opposite of love.

Fear is the opposite of love: take a moment to consider this idea. Most people think of hate as the opposite of love. But now consider the possibility that love cannot truly coexist with fear.

Each day this week, take the time to write down the things that make you feel afraid. How do you feel when you are afraid? What are the underlying messages of your fear? When you are afraid, what specifically do you anticipate happening?

Perhaps you may find on your list these thoughts: "When I meet someone that I care about, I am afraid that she will not care about me," or "when I make love to my partner, I am afraid that I cannot please him." In each of these situations, the fear expressed is of not being good enough. These feelings of unworthiness keep us closed and defensive. We cannot express ourselves from a loving place when we are afraid.

This week, remember that when you are afraid of not

being good enough, you are not accepting and loving yourself as you are. Truly loving and accepting yourself will also have an effect on the way people feel and relate to you. Realize that other people will love you to the same degree that you love yourself. This week, begin to accept yourself by saying: "I am good enough just the way I am," as you look in the mirror each morning.

If I were a man/If I
were a woman...

This week, give yourself permission to take a risk: Think about what it's like to be a member of the opposite sex. While you are imagining this, many judgments may arise, as well as some scary feelings. Be gentle with yourself and allow these thoughts to occur. This is a time for you to explore not only your feelings about the other sex, but your feelings about yourself. As you observe the opposite sex, write down your impressions. How do they move? Can you imagine what it would feel like to be in one of their bodies? How do they occupy space? What impressions do they give you?

As you begin to imagine yourself as a member of the opposite sex, you might feel a lot of tenderness—or you might have angry emotions. Try not to judge your feelings. If you are doing this exercise with a partner, it might help to share your feelings with him or her.

Now visualize what your body would look and feel like if you were of the opposite sex. Would you be the same height? Would you be as big? As small? How would these differences make you feel? Go through every part of your body—your head, your hair, your face—and visualize the physical changes that might occur. How would it feel to have facial hair, or to shave it off? How would it feel to put on makeup? Do this with every part of your body. How would you walk, sit, and move? Do these physical changes create emotional changes? How do you feel right now as you think about this? Do you feel apprehensive, or fearful, curious, or excited?

Above all, accept whatever you are feeling. Acknowledge your courage and imagination in exploring these questions—and then go on. What are some of the benefits of being of the opposite sex? What are the negative factors? Is there anything that you have never realized before? Spend some time each day exploring these questions as an adventure in getting to know the opposite sex.

Now ask yourself: What did I learn about *myself* this week by thinking about being a different gender?

Sex is fun.

Sex is fun. How come they never taught you that at home or in school? If you really do not consider sex fun, perhaps you have become too concerned about how you perform in bed, or too worried about how your body looks, or too caught up in what your partner thinks of you. You might even be worried about what your parent might think. No wonder you can't have fun, if you carry all these worries to bed. If all you do is worry, you will miss out on the joy of sex.

No lion ever worries about "not being good enough," or that he is "bad" for having sex. For animals, sexual issues are much simpler: When they're hot, they're hot, and when they're not, they're not.

This week, if you are having sex, or fantasizing, just let go of your worries. Don't be judgmental about what you are doing or try to force what is happening. Just relax and have fun. Sex is a celebration. Listen to your body and follow its movements. Let your body be an expression of your total being—and your joyfulness.

You can even try some silly things to help lighten up your lovemaking. Tickling is one way to loosen up an encounter that has become too serious. It is also a great way to begin foreplay. What about playing strip poker or pretending you are children playing doctor? You also could try your hand at body painting. If you use your imagination and let go, you'll come up with some of your own techniques for increasing the fun in your sex life.

I will have no more "shoulds."

More often than not, it isn't other people that keep us from enjoying a satisfying sex life, but rather our own belief system. We are often deprived of joy by an inner voice that tells us how we should or should not act. The problem is that this inner voice only hears "I have to" and "I should"—never "I want to" or "I need," which are at the center of a fulfilling sex life. Here are some common "I shoulds" that inhibit the sexual experience:

- I should want to make love every time my partner does.
- I should be able to have an orgasm every time we make love.
- I should never think about wanting to have sex with someone else.
- I should be more responsive sexually.

You can probably add many other "I shoulds" of your own to this list.

23

This week, make a list of the "I shoulds" that keep you from enjoying your sexual experience, and spend time thinking about them. Focus on the idea that you have the power to eliminate these barriers to sexual pleasure. After all, you created them. All you have to do is give yourself permission to have a fulfilling sex life. With that in mind, at the end of the week, replace your list with a list of "I want tos." Notice how this new perspective feels—relieved, free, excited. Now you'll be able to appreciate how your sexual behavior has been affected by each of your beliefs about how you "should" be. Finally, tear up your list of "shoulds" and resolve not to draw up any more. Give yourself permission to be just the way you are.

I know how to speak sexually.

When the lights are low and you are with that certain person, or when you are getting into a "heavy" discussion about sex, how do you express yourself? For a discussion to be meaningful, you must communicate in the same language and on the same level. This is even more true when you are talking about sex.

Some people refer to parts of the body by their scientific names: penis, vagina, breasts. Others use childhood words: peewee, weewee, titties. Still others use street language: cock, cunt, jugs. Each of these styles imparts a different flavor and communicates a different meaning. Do you feel comfortable talking about sex in any of these ways?

Imagine yourself making love to someone—touching and caressing every part of his or her body. Visualize everything you are doing with him or her. Now describe it verbally. What words have you chosen? Do you feel comfortable with them? Try using a different sexual vocabulary to describe your action. Does using different words change how you feel sexually? If you are used to using sexual slang, using the medical terminology may awaken a hidden respect for sex. On the other hand, if you are very formal and use only scientific terminology, trying some slang may loosen you up and turn you on. Use childhood words where you never had before—it may awaken a sense of innocence. If you totally avoid the use of sexual terminology, beginning to speak sexually may be a freeing and stimulating experience.

This week, try different ways of expressing yourself sexually. Have fun expanding your language, and then try sharing it with a partner. How you speak sexually is another way of communicating who you are.

I deserve to receive love.

One of the greatest gifts you can give yourself is to open your heart and feel your worthiness to receive love. In this moment, you give a gift to yourself and your partner, and the giver and the receiver become one.

This may seem to be the opposite of what we were taught as children: that it is better to give than to receive. But it is not. Many of us have come to believe that fulfilling your own wants and needs means being greedy and selfish. Can you remember a time when you felt guilty because you wanted something for yourself, or wanted to do something that others didn't want to do? We have been programmed to believe that unless we give to others to the exclusion of our own needs, we are bad.

The truth is that loving is giving, both to others and to yourself. But before you can truly give to others, you have to give to yourself. If you cannot give yourself what you need, when you need it, and if you believe that doing for others is more important than doing for yourself, there must be a place in you that feels unworthy to receive. It is this belief in your own unworthiness that dictates the lack of success of your relationships. If a person cannot give to himself, he will, in the long run, be limited in his giving to others.

How will this affect your sexual relationships? Imagine a time when you are making love. Take all the time you need. Focus the images. How do you see yourself? If you are basically passive, do you feel guilty about it? Do you end up on the receiving end, but never feel fully satisfied, because you are afraid to ask for what you really want? Or do you find yourself constantly giving to your partner and never getting around to fulfilling your needs? These actions may be created by the belief that it is better to give than to receive. In either case, this belief leads to a feeling of being perpetually deprived and in need of nurturing and attention. Now change channels and see yourself as an active receiver. How does it feel to receive? If you feel uncomfortable, what are some of the thoughts running through your mind? Be specific. Perhaps you would like to write them down.

After imagining what it would be like, see if you can arrange an encounter with your sexual partner for the express purpose of receiving affection and attention. Give yourself permission to ask for what you want, and to luxuriate completely in all you are receiving. After it is over, notice how full you feel and how ready you are to give to others from a place of satisfaction rather than obligation.

I have the right to say no.

□

This week's thought, the right to say no, will help you to feel okay about saying no. It will help you understand that to be able to say no is to create boundaries for yourself, to set limits where others are concerned, to acknowledge and claim your own needs. Your inability to say no can become mixed up with the feelings of the child in you, who needs approval and acceptance; if it does, learning to say no can start to free you of that demanding child.

As children, most of us have been taught that to say no is selfish, inconsiderate, and unloving. We have learned that if we wanted something other than what our parents wanted, we earned their anger, disapproval, and the loss of their love. When you explore this week's thought, know that each time you are afraid to say no, you are trapped in your child's belief that if you say no, you will lose the approval of the "authority." When you believe you have the right to say no, you are approving your own desires. You have begun to take responsibility for your own pleasure.

Now examine how that child's fear to say no influences your sexual relationship. Remember a time when you wanted to say no to someone regarding some aspect of your sexual relationship. You wanted to say no, and yet you didn't. What were you feeling? What were your judgments against yourself? What were the rational reasons you gave yourself for saying yes? How did you feel about yourself? Allow yourself to explore other times, other experiences, when you wanted to say no, to set limits, or support what you needed, and yet you were afraid to do so. See that there is a part of you that believes that if you say no, you will lose love. The reality is that saying no when you want supports your own belief in your worthiness.

This week, practice saying into the mirror, "I have the right to say no." Say it until you believe it. Repeat to yourself, "In saying no, I am meeting my own needs." Then practice with your sexual partner. The next time you feel like saying no, risk saying it. Although you may have to deal with some discomfort at first, you will feel an integrity and self-respect that make it all worthwhile.

Ladies and Gentlemen
—introducing your
genitals.

The road to sexual fulfillment includes the thoughts, the attitudes, the socialization, the religious beliefs, and a most-often ignored knowledge and understanding of sexual organs.

Many of us feel embarrassment or shame about our genitals. This week's thought may provide you with a safe space to get to know and understand this part of your anatomy that has been both praised and maligned in almost every art form.

Many people who have been engaged in sexual activity have never taken the time to explore their own or their partner's genitalia. To many, the sexual organs appear neither appealing nor sexy. This week we will explore our judgments, feelings, and attitudes about your genitals.

As we begin this exploration, notice how you are feeling. If you are feeling nervous, allow yourself some time to relax and become receptive to this exercise, which is an adventure in getting to know the most intimate part of your anatomy. Start your exploration with a warm bath or shower. As you bathe yourself, ask yourself these questions:

- Do I feel comfortable touching myself? What are some of the injunctions from the past that come up now?
- When I do touch my genitals, do I like the smell, the taste? How do I think I should smell or taste?
- What are some of the thoughts and associations that come up for you? Do you remember jokes or comments about your genitals that make you feel ashamed? What are they?
- If you were to allow yourself an image of your genitals, what would it be? If you are a man, is it perhaps a cannon—if a woman, a peach or a flower?

You may have more thoughts about your genitals. Allow them to surface. If you are choosing to do this exploring with a partner, share your feelings. You may want to share childhood memories about self-exploration or perhaps the first time you mutually explored your genitals with a friend. These exercises may bring up many feelings. Be open and soft with each other.

Now we will move to another step of self-exploration. Find a place where you will not be disturbed and where you will be comfortable and warm. You will need a hand mirror and a pad and pencil. Remove your clothes. Remember when you were in elementary school and you had show and tell? This is what we are going to do now. Begin to look at your genitals. What do you see? You may want to write this or just speak it out loud: My genitals are _____. Looking at them, I feel _____. I was surprised that _____.

Now, draw a picture of your genitals. You do not have to be an artist—just allow your creativity to take over. When you have finished, look at your drawing and then at your genitals. What are you feeling now? What have you learned about your genitals, and about yourself? Our genitals are as unique as our faces. Are you willing to love this part of yourself? If not, what judgments keep you from doing so? After acknowledging these judgments, try to counteract them by simply affirming, "I love all of me, including my genitals." You will feel better about yourself for it.

I can feel good about
pleasuring myself.

The *Random House Dictionary of the English Language* defines masturbation as "the stimulation or manipulation of one's own genitals resulting in an orgasm; sexual self-gratification." The art of self-pleasuring has been a practice that has been written about in many ancient cultures. Yet for many years, the practice has been joked about and long been derided as an expression of sexuality.

There are many superstitions and old wives' tales about masturbation. Some people say that it weakens you, while others say that it's a juvenile habit. At one time, it was said that it would make you go blind. Let's explore some of the myths, beliefs, and information that you carry around with you about self-pleasuring.

Of the many old wives' tales, which have you chosen to believe? Write them down on a piece of paper. Do not judge them, just take a mental inventory, and ask yourself, "Does this thought support my pleasure?" The purpose of this week's seed thought, "I can feel good about pleasuring myself," is meant to give you the time and space to explore your own thinking and feeling about the subject.

Now go back to the first time that you can remember touching your body. How old are you? What are you feeling? Is it pleasure? Do you feel naughty? Did someone catch you? How did they make you feel? Take all the time you need to explore these memories.

Now take a moment to check out your body. Do you feel tense as you go through this exercise? Breathe into where you are holding the tension. That's it, relax and breathe. Remind yourself that you are giving yourself permission to explore your past conditioning so that you will be able to participate fully in the self-pleasuring, the self-celebration. Know that whatever feelings come up for you are okay. If you acknowledge these feelings and understand the circumstances surrounding this first masturbatory experience, it will lead to a greater awareness of who you are sexually.

After you have done this exploration, review your attitudes about self-pleasuring by completing this statement:

Self-pleasuring is _____.

Fill in this blank as many times as you need to understand what you feel. If you fill in the blank with a negative belief, try to let go of it.

Know that by giving yourself pleasure and taking responsibility for the release of your own sexual tensions, you are liberating yourself. There are many times when we cannot be with a partner, but that does not mean that we cannot have pleasure. Masturbation is an act of independence. It allows you to take responsibility for orgasm, whether you are alone or with a partner. The more you know, the better you are able to let go of taboos, old wives' tales, and to give yourself permission to enjoy and celebrate your sexual self.

I free myself from ideas of normal and planned sexuality.

Normal, as defined in the dictionary, refers to a standard or pattern regarded as "typical or usual." Therefore, abnormal refers to "one whose behavior differs from acceptable social standards." Consider for a moment what pressures we then place upon ourselves to accept the standards of others to be "normal" in our sexual behavior.

In every society, there are rules that govern sexual standards. These rules dictate the norms. It is important to be aware that sexuality is cultural, and what is acceptable in one country may be inappropriate in another. In some countries, kissing on the mouth is not the norm; in others, nudity is accepted. In the United States, certain sexual practices are outlawed in some states but not in others. Religious practices also dictate our sexuality. Some religious communities practice polygamy. The norm is decided by our geography, economics, and religion: it is not solely a function of biology.

If you were brought up in a home where kissing and

touching were the norm, you might have difficulty in a relationship with someone who was brought up to feel that this display of public affection was offensive. If your family's norm was to consider premarital sex a natural and happy consequence of a loving relationship, then you might have negative judgments about someone who did not take part in it. *Normal* is a function of how we were taught. *Abnormal* is what deviates from these standards. Consider how you have come to judge yourself and others based on variations of cultural teachings. In doing this you may give yourself permission to enjoy a freer, more expanded sexual reality.

Each day this week, allow yourself time to be quiet. Search your mind for your judgments about "being normal." Explore the web of your belief systems that make your way *right* and the other *wrong* or that causes you to judge yourself for having desires you believe are abnormal. Do this as openly as possible.

Now try letting go of some of these beliefs, and notice how you feel about it. The more open and less judgmental you allow yourself to be, the sooner you will be able to enjoy the pleasure of your sexuality, in any way you choose.

I know and appreciate
my body.

☐

Let us take this week to see how you feel about your body. Much of our image of the ideal body comes from the media. What we see in the magazines, on television, and in the movies influences us greatly. We begin to compare ourselves to the ideals set for us, and of course, most of us suffer from the comparison. It would be wonderful if we could look into the mirror and see ourselves without judgment, and without comparison. This week we will attempt to do just that.

Choose one or two nights this week to try the following exercise. Since you will be exploring your body, you might like to take a shower before you begin. Then put on some music that you enjoy and lower the lights.

Stand naked in front of a mirror. Allow yourself to be a friendly witness . . . do not judge yourself. Think "I am my body." Now look at your feet, your legs, your thighs . . . go through each part of your body. Touch yourself, explore yourself, as if this were the first time you were seeing yourself. Becoming aware of how your body looks, feels, and smells. Take the time to enjoy this exploration. Do you like what you see?

Now bring your judgments and beliefs out into the open. Pretend that you are introducing your body to a group of people. How are you feeling? Are you nervous thinking that people are seeing you nude? What do you like about your body? Take all the time you need. Do you like your hair, its color? Do you like the feel of your skin? Your feet? What about your legs and your buttocks? Do you like the hair on your pubic mound? Take in your body slowly. What are your beliefs and judgments about it?

Write a list of all the things you like about your physical self. Start at the top of your head, and slowly, slowly look and see who you are. You may not be perfect, you may not be your idealized image, but can you accept yourself just the way you are? The person who is really considered sexual is the one who accepts and enjoys himself, and does not feel ashamed of who he is.

Take one more long look in the mirror. That's it, look into your own eyes. Begin to accept your body the way it is. Try visualizing making love to your body. Try loving yourself. Finish this week's exercise by repeating to yourself, "It may not be perfect, but I love and appreciate my body."

I know what excites me and turns me on.

Turning each other on is a very important part of "making love." If you are not aroused physically, mentally, and sensually, you will not be stimulated to make love. To take your sexual experience out of the ordinary and the mechanical, you have to know what feels good to you.

Remember when you are taking a journey, getting there is half the fun. Take some time each evening this week to explore what turns you on. First, remember a time when you were turned on. What did you feel? Did your heart beat faster? Did you feel weak? Did your body sing? Did you feel warm and cuddly? Did you want more? Identify these feelings. Take all the time you need. Remember what your body felt like. Remember what you were thinking. Now you know how you feel when you are turned on.

The next part of this exercise is to consider the sensual things that turn you on. You may want to make a list of these things. Do you feel turned on in the morning? Does sunshine turn you on? Is it the smell of perfume or clean linens or the smell of a pipe? Does it feel good to have your genitals touched or your earlobes caressed?

Now consider the thoughts that excite you. Mental stimulation is an important ingredient for making happy love. Each of us has different sexual memories that may arouse us. For some of us, our darkest beliefs about sex are the most exciting. Perhaps sex with a married person, or your boss, or the thought of playing with yourself while someone watches is what does it for you. Do not judge yourself. Just see what excites you most.

It is also very important to note who turns you on: We all have images of the type of person we are attracted to. The clearer you are about who, where, and what, the more fun you will have and the more satisfaction you will receive.

Now that you know the things that will arouse you sexually, try arranging for one of them this week. Either ask a partner to help you out or create an experience for yourself. Then let yourself luxuriate in the warmth of your sexual appetite.

Foreplay is the
doorway to pleasure.

This week we will explore foreplay. This is the stuff of which movies are made. It's the tasty, juicy first stages of a sexual experience. It's a time of playful arousal and tender caresses. This is the part of sex where desire is awakened, when longing is built to a peak. It is what is often so wonderful about a new sexual encounter—that initial exploration and absorption in the body of your partner at a luxurious pace. Sadly, it's also the first thing that goes in long-term sexual relationships. When you know each other well, the easy thing to do is to hop into bed and within minutes, have intercourse and orgasm. What a loss of pleasure! Foreplay is essential for heightened sexual pleasure, because the more you build sexual tension, the greater your release will be. So this week, we will concentrate on reawakening the pleasures of foreplay, the pleasures of turning each other on.

First of all, give yourself enough time. Foreplay should not be a frantic groping for a buildup of sexual charge but a slow, delicious arousal. Next take the time to discover what aspects of foreplay really work for you. Everybody's different, so learn to know what you like and what your partner likes.

Now here are suggestions for a few techniques you may want to try. Kissing. Imagine yourself kissing your partner. How do you make contact? Kissing is an erotic expression and can be highly stimulating. Do you use your tongue? Do you nibble and suck? Do you know that in some cultures people kiss by rubbing noses or sniffing? Do you limit your kissing to the mouth? Can you imagine yourself kissing other parts of the body? How do you feel about this thought? Allow yourself to explore in your imagination what it feels like to kiss the neck, the ears, the back, the breasts. Oral contact does not have to be limited to the mouth. Another type of kiss is the genital kiss. Although oral-genital stimulation has become much more widespread, it may not feel right for you. What are your thoughts about it? Allow yourself to explore them. Above all, remember, don't engage in this activity if you don't feel comfortable with it.

Touching and receiving pleasure are the most important parts of foreplay. The body is a temple to be explored, to be tasted, to be enjoyed, not to be invaded or violated. Have you explored tickling, biting, gentle pinching? Using your hands, your lips, to explore the sensitive parts of the body are all parts of foreplay. Allow yourself to be imaginative and playful. Some people like to spank and to play at being naughty with one being the parent and one partner being the child. Allow yourself to imagine yourself playing out some game if you both are turned on to it.

You are safe to explore what you like, what feels good, and what doesn't. Do not judge yourself. Sex is an expression of self, and foreplay is an expression of your complete feeling of your sexual union. Reawaken your appreciation of this luxurious process, and delight in it.

Freeing my pelvis leads to greater sexual pleasure.

☐

Sexual functioning depends in part on a free-moving pelvis. Since the activity of sex involves moving the pelvis, the freer and less tense this area of the body is, the more pleasure we will derive from our sexual encounters.

Most of us in this culture have what is referred to as a "frozen pelvis." From the time we are children we learn to tighten the muscles in the pelvic area in order to hide our sexuality or protect ourselves from experiencing sexual feelings. There are many reasons for this. We may have been taught that our sexual feelings were bad or shameful, or perhaps we had a seductive mother or father from whom we felt we had to protect ourselves. We may simply have not had a proper sexual education and therefore felt frightened of the feelings streaming through us. In each of these cases our solution was to freeze our pelvic girdle in order to decrease the flow of sexual energy and excitement there.

The pelvis is a mirror for sexual attitudes. If it is held tight and stiff, it indicates some resistance or inability to experience a full spectrum of sexual feelings. Even if you have overcome your sexual inhibitions on the mental and emotional level, your pelvic muscles, which have been in chronic contraction for years, may still be holding tight.

This week, we will work to free up our pelvises, to make them fluid and alive again, to allow them to be dynamic receptacles for the free flow of our sexual energy. Begin by standing in front of a mirror in a natural position. Become as comfortable as you can. Find your pelvis by placing your hands on your hipbones. Now become aware of how this area looks and feels. Is it pulled back or thrust forward? Does your pelvis feel tight or rigid? Now start moving your pelvis in a wide circular movement, as if you were standing in a round room, trying to get your pelvis to reach out and touch the walls. Stretch it to the side, then the front, then to the other side, then to the back, really stretch and move your pelvis. How does it feel? Now place your hands on your hips. What statement is your body making? Your body posture comes from your mind's attitude. What attitude is your body expressing? Just be playful—no judgments. Move your pelvis around, slowly, provocatively. There's no one watching, unless you are doing this exercise with your partner. Let yourself have fun; tease, seduce. Don't hold back; let everything stored in your pelvis come out.

Is there a sound stored in your pelvis? Is there some movement that you have been holding in, holding back? Are there words that go along with the movements? Say them aloud. Now really begin to thrust and move your pelvis. Keep your knees bent, and keep breathing.

As your pelvis thrusts forward, feel the pleasure. Move it forward and say yes; then move it back and say no. Practice the words with the movement, and just allow yourself to feel the power in each position. How does it feel to let your pelvis talk and move? This is a fun exercise to explore with a partner. Try moving your pelvis every day this week. It will help you let go of any old feelings you are holding there, and it will help increase your range of sexual movement. The freer the pelvis, the more capacity you have for sexual pleasure and fun.

Vibrators can be liberating.

Vibrators can be a wonderful tool for enhancing your sexual experience and improving your sexual responsiveness.

Most of us have seen vibrators or at least are familiar with what they are. They come in a variety of shapes and sizes. Some are made for massage but can be effectively used for sexual pleasure. They may be in the shape of a penis or have various attachments such as vibrating tips or rotating disks.

To use a vibrator, simply place it directly over or near the genitals. The wonderful thing about vibrators is that the user can control the pressure and placement so as to receive exactly the right amount of stimulation. The fact that they vibrate rhythmically can help you to surrender to the rhythmic forces needed to build up to a successful orgasm. And since they never grow tired, you have all the time you need to get enough stimulation to reach climax.

Vibrators can be especially helpful to women who have difficulty reaching orgasm. The intensity of the vibrations is hard to resist, making orgasm more likely. Once a woman has become orgasmic through using a vibrator, she will find it easier to repeat the experience, either through lovemaking with a partner or through other forms of masturbation.

A vibrator can also enhance the lovemaking pleasures for couples. For example, a man can enter his lover's vagina from behind while either he or she applies the vibrator to her clitoris. The sensations she experiences will cause more intense vaginal contractions, which will directly give more pleasure to her man.

The vibrator can be applied to the man's penis as well for increased sensation and enjoyment. Or you can use it over different parts of the body to enliven your entire sexual encounter.

Since vibrators can be fun and are so helpful, what stops us from taking full advantage of the pleasures they can provide? First of all, there is a myth that vibrators are harmful because they can become addictive, spoiling a person for any other kind of sex. This is absolutely untrue. A vibrator only helps to free up sexual flow and response. Second, many of us feel guilty or ashamed of using something mechanical during sex. Don't be—the important thing about sex is giving and receiving pleasure. If vibrators help, don't hesitate to use them. The third reason is not knowing where to buy one or feeling too embarrassed to go to a store that sells them. This problem can be solved by ordering from a magazine (most pornographic magazines advertise vibrators). Better yet, know that the salesperson in your local sex boutique is used to dealing with people's embarrassment. They are completely matter-of-fact about the whole thing and will help you feel more at ease. Just get up the courage to walk in and make your purchase. You have a better chance of acquiring the vibrator best suited to you if you can see your choices and get some good advice from the salesperson. If you cannot muster the courage to do either of these, go to your local drugstore and ask for a back and neck vibrator.

This week, if you have a vibrator, find time to use it, either by yourself or with your partner. Explore what makes you feel good. Experiment and have fun. If you don't own a vibrator, this is the week to purchase one. Then give it a try. Use it in any way that gives you pleasure. Just remember, it's an electric device, so stay away from bathtubs, hot tubs, and showers.

What to do if I'm just not turned on.

How often do you feel that you're just not turned on? How do you feel about yourself at those times? Most of us feel some concern when we are not turned on. We begin to question whether something might be wrong with us. We may even begin to blame our partners. In many cases, of course, there is nothing amiss. We are just in a natural cycle and need to honor our own sexual rhythms. In other cases, especially if we are not feeling sexually aroused for prolonged periods, we owe it to ourselves to know what the causes might be.

Some of the reasons for not being turned on are very simple. Are you on any medication? Drugs, both prescription and over-the-counter, may be affecting you. If you are on any drugs, consult your physician as to their effects on sexual arousal. Any illness, even the flu, may affect your sexual desire. In this case, just accept the fact that you may be run-down. Give yourself time to nurture yourself or your partner by cuddling and touching, without demanding that you be sexual. Another rather obvious reason for inhibited sexual desire is the fear of pregnancy. Are you taking proper birth control precautions? Do you know about them? Check with a doctor or a birth control clinic. Some older people believe sexuality should diminish with age. They are therefore ashamed of their still-vibrant sexual feelings and try to deny them. Is this your issue? Another cause for sexual uninterest is that it may be painful. If that is the reason, discuss this with your partner. Perhaps he needs to be more gentle. Going to a doctor for a physical examination may reveal a reason for the pain. Do not suffer in silence—it may be very simple to clear up.

Another reason for people "turning off" is work overload and fatigue. This is especially true of mothers of young children or overscheduled businesspeople. After a busy and stressful day, it is often difficult to summon up sexual desire. Sometimes too many responsibilities leave one with very little sexual energy. Perhaps you feel unsexual because you are trying to make yourself invulnerable so as to avoid feeling hurt or taken advantage of. It might be that you are angry with your partner and are therefore withholding sex from him or her. If this is the case, work out your anger another way. You are only punishing yourself when you deaden your sexuality. There could also be deeper psychological issues at fault. It could be guilt about sex, feelings of shame about one's body, or even a repressed memory of sexual abuse.

This week, take note of how often you feel turned off. If it is a chronic problem, see if some of the reasons mentioned here seem to apply. Then take some action to change the situation. If it is a more deeply rooted psychological problem, perhaps the time has come to seek some form of counseling.

Sex is one of life's greatest pleasures. Don't let yourself become apathetic about the loss of your sexual appetite. Do whatever you need to do to reawaken your sexual desire.

My sexual fantasies are a banquet.

Sexual fantasies are a banquet. They are an opportunity to explore your desires and imagination. What are your secret fantasies? This week, have a fantasy feast. When we go into a restaurant, most of us know what type of food we like. We never ask ourselves why we like French food or prefer Chinese food. We just know that we have choices. So should it be with sexual appetites and fantasies. We should be able to taste freely from the table of delicacies, allowing ourselves to enjoy fully our choices.

This week, we will begin to explore our secret fantasy banquet. As we do, we will discover that great pleasures await us from the world of our imaginations. The only things holding us back from the deliciousness of our own sexual imaginings are self-judgment and guilt.

So let's begin by absolving ourselves. Your sexual fantasies, whatever they may be, are okay, and you are okay for having them. They come from your own private world, and because they are fantasies, they have no power to hurt you or anyone else. Although sexual fantasies can be looked at psychologically to discover a person's inner anger or pain, this is not our aim this week. We simply want to give ourselves permission to explore the full scope of our fantasy world—to allow ourselves to be turned on by our own sexual imaginations, with no holds barred. When we do this, we allow ourselves to be fully stimulated and actually clear the way for more satisfaction in all areas of our sex lives. We become freer, less guilt-ridden, more likely to experiment. We learn how to flow with the full pleasure of our sexuality.

With this in mind, set aside some time each day to explore your secret garden of fantasies. Be sure that you are alone and will be uninterrupted so that you can take the time to allow your fantasies to unwind.

What situations turn you on? Be specific. Know everything about the time, the environment, the person, or persons. Do not limit yourself by your fears or your judgments. What are the words that turn you on, what sexcapades does your mind create? Is your secret fantasy a desire for a threesome, or a one-night stand with someone of the same sex? Perhaps it is some form of exhibitionism or voyeurism? Maybe it is a scene where you are taken by force or tied down. Still another scenario might be a passionate love affair with an adored lover. Your fantasy may include group sex or sex with a forbidden person. The possibilities are endless. If you have trouble summoning up fantasies of your own, try buying a book of sexual fantasies (you will find several to choose from in any well-stocked bookstore) or looking at a pornographic magazine. Discover what appeals to you, and allow it to stimulate your own sexual visions.

You may find that these fantasies make you want to masturbate. Go ahead. Give yourself as much pleasure as you can stand. You may feel you want to share your fantasies with your partner. This can make for a very exciting and satisfying evening of sexual pleasure. Just make sure that you leave your guilt and self-judgment outside the door to your sexual imagination. Then enjoy the banquet. *Bon appetit!*

My partner and I take turns "going first."

Do you worry about not being able to have an orgasm? Or are you afraid that you will reach orgasm too quickly, and then your partner will be unhappy? Do you judge that it takes you too long to have an orgasm and that your partner may get "bored." Do you spend a lot of time worrying about who goes first and what your partner is thinking?

This is a concern for many lovers. "I take too long, you take too little time, and how are we ever going to 'come' together?" This week we are going to let go of some of this pressure and this internal dialogue about orgasm.

First of all, think of an exciting or different way to choose who is going to go first. It may be the last person who paid for dinner this week, or the person who had the roughest week, or the person who is wearing red. Let your imagination find a creative way to choose.

"You go first" means that this evening all the attention, the loving, and sexual consciousness is to be on YOU. Both partners are concentrating on the one who goes first.

Allow yourself to play, to give, to receive, to flow, to be in the moment. All tension is off; all minds are at complete peak pleasuring. What you will truly enjoy about this exercise is that it is so filled with pleasuring that any tension about having an orgasm is released.

This exercise is really a gift to both partners, but if you go first, have a wonderful evening. Remember to set a date for switching who goes first.

I understand the human sexual response cycle.

When we want to do something, build something, make something, cook something, we usually take some time to learn about what it is and how to go about it. There are four stages to making love, and it is my belief that if you know and understand these cycles, some of the mysteries, or even disappointments, about your sexual experiences may be cleared up. Knowing about the human sexual response system can help make your sexual experiences more pleasurable.

The first stage is the *excitement stage*. This is when the initial reaction to stimulus takes place, and foreplay has begun. There is a physical excitation in both partners: penis and clitoris become erect, nipples harden, breathing quickens, and a lubricating substance is emitted. In other words, this is when all systems are steaming up.

The next stage is the *plateau stage*, when the tension and the pressure build. Everything increases in this stage. The tissues around the vagina begin to swell, which allows for the penis to be taken in, the testes in the male move closer to his body, and excitation is concentrated in the genitals. There is a pulsating and thrusting movement of the pelvis, and it is now that all systems are on "go."

This stage spills into the next stage. This buildup of tension, of involuntary movement, of letting go, is the *orgasm*, or *release*, *stage*. This is the moment over which there is no control, the moment both of you have been waiting for. Intense involuntary contractions take place in the musculature of the uterus, vagina, and clitoris and in the penis, and the man ejaculates. This experience is also referred to as "coming," climaxing, letting go.

The final stage of the human sexual response cycle is the *resolution*. At this point, the man feels totally relaxed and satisfied. No matter what the temptation or stimulation, most men, after ejaculation, cannot respond. The penis becomes flaccid, and the man usually becomes sleepy. The woman's body may take as long as a half hour to return to the same state as before lovemaking began. It is this stage that is very different for a man and a woman. A woman can be stimulated again to reach orgasm, and she does not appear to need as long a recovery period as a man. This idea may be useful the next time you make love; it can help you to understand that the difference is not lack of desire but the physiological differences between the male and female bodies.

Learning about the human response cycle can help you understand the mechanics of making love so that as the stages appear, you can let go and flow with the movements. You can take full pleasure in each stage, knowing that the more time and energy you give to each, the more fulfilling your sexual experience will be.

I can relax and let go.

"**R**elax; why don't you relax?"

Have you ever heard someone say that to you? Perhaps you would relax, if you could. Relaxing your mind and your body is a very important prelude to making love. The more relaxed you are, the more open you are to the flow of sexual energy through your body. More sexual energy traveling through your system means greater pleasure and excitement. This week we will take some time to learn how to relax.

What follows is one of the oldest and best body relaxation exercises. This exercise can be done alone or with your partner. Try taping it. Then simply play it back. This may make it easier for you to surrender to a deep level of relaxation.

Wear loose clothing. Take your phone off the hook. Lie on your back on the floor. Make sure you are comfortable. Feel the rug or the floor underneath you. Allow your body to settle in. Close your eyes. This exercise requires at least twenty minutes for maximum results.

Become aware of your breathing. Just follow it. Feel it fill your lungs. Feel your chest move as your breath goes in and out. Coming in . . . going out . . . breathing in . . . breathing out . . . coming in like the tide, going out like the tide; just a gentle motion of in and out. Let this rhythm take over for a while. Relax . . . inhale and exhale and let go . . . relax and let go. . . .

Now start with your toes. Tighten them, curl them . . . curl and feel and tighten every toe . . . hold . . . hold . . . tighter . . . tighter . . . and now . . . let go.

Now tense your feet, tighten the arches, the soles; tighten, tighter . . . and let go.

Continue upward to your legs . . . tighten so that your toes, your feet, your legs, become stiff, tense, like two iron rods . . . hold . . . hold . . . tighter . . . then breathe and let go.

Now tense your entire leg, including your knees, your thighs . . . tighter, tense, holding, tighter . . . until they hurt, and with a big exhalation, let go.

Now tense your feet, your ankles, your legs, your thighs, and your buttocks and genitals . . . hold them as tightly as you can, tensing, holding, tighter . . . still tighter, hold, and then with a swoosh of breath, let go. Relax. Good.

Now move up your back, tightening from the tip of your toes, up, up, through your buttocks, genitals, and the lower back, and each vertebra, holding, as if a rod were up your back, tighter, tighter, your shoulders, tense, and stiff . . . hold, hold; don't give in . . . hold . . . tighter . . . then breathe and let go.

As you continue moving up your body, tighten every part that has been mentioned. Now include your neck, your upper arms, and your lower arms and fingers. Everything

is stiff, tight, and you hold, hold, hold, until you let go
. . . and breathe, letting the breath fill you up.

Now tighten every part of you, including your face.
Tense around the mouth, pushing the lips forward, the jaw,
holding tightly the cheeks, around the eyes, the forehead
. . . hold . . . tighten. Every part of your body is tensed,
held, squeezed . . . hold, hold . . . don't let go. And then,
when you can hang on no longer . . . breathe. Let out your
breath through your mouth with a swooshing sound, and
allow every part of you to go limp, melt, become one with
the floor. No bones, no muscles, just like melted butter.
Follow your breath . . . no mind . . . no body, just the
breath. Relax and let go.

Notice how you feel after you've completed this exercise. Are there areas that you simply could not relax? If so,
don't worry—it takes practice. For most of us, relaxation
is something that must be learned. Try this exercise at least
twice this week. If you're doing this with a partner, as an
extra treat culminate the experience with making love. Discover the mutual joys of relaxing and letting go.

Touching me,
touching you.

For some of us, making love can become an exclusively genital act. This week, the seed thought is "touching me, touching you." The idea is to experience the entire body as your sexual organ. To become aware of every inch of it, of areas that you normally do not even know are there. As you go through this immensely pleasurable experience, you will awaken to the subtleties and wonder of your own body, as well as your partner's. The next time you make love, you may have the heightened experience of feeling your entire body involved in the process.

The following exercise is designed to help bring you this new awareness of your body. It involves allowing yourself permission to lie back and be totally given to.

Set aside ten minutes for each partner, create a comfortable place to lie down in, and add some soft music and lights if you wish.

After you have arranged the "setting," one of you will lie with no clothes on and make him- or herself comfortable. This person will be the receiver. The other will be the giver. Do not speak, although you may make appreciative sounds. The giver will then explore the receiver's body from head to toe with just one fingertip, gently stroking and exploring, as if sensing the partner for the very first time. The idea is to stroke and cover every inch of the skin gently. The suggestion is that you spend at least five minutes on the front of the body, and then ask your partner to turn over. Do not be surprised if you want more time.

When you have completed this loving exploration, hold each other silently for a few seconds, remembering that this is a nonverbal process. Then change positions. After each partner has been a receiver, you might like to share your experiences.

You may, of course, wish to do this exercise by yourself. It is no less pleasurable and can in fact be very enlightening, as you allow yourself to explore areas of your own body you have never before paid attention to. Whether alone or with a partner, you can add to this experience by using silk, feathers, or furs to explore your body. Use your imagination. Touching me, touching you can be a moving experience. Treat this exercise seriously and it will help you to develop a new reverence for your body and all the pleasures it contains.

Withheld anger decreases sexual enjoyment.

☐

Withheld anger can cause some problems, both to you and to your partner. First of all, in order to stop your anger from escaping, you make yourself rigid. A tremendous amount of energy goes toward creating these impenetrable walls. Not only does this rigidity create internal stress on your mind and body, it prohibits the relaxed and spontaneous flow of energy you need for fulfilling lovemaking. Even so, because you are human, you cannot possibly erect foolproof barricades, so you are in constant danger of springing anger leaks. These take the form of hostility, cruelty, and criticism, which may seep out unexpectedly onto your partner. Worse yet, you may push your anger so deep within you that you hate yourself and become depressed. How can a person who has collapsed under the weight of such a burden possibly summon the energy for sex, let alone feel she deserves the pleasure?

This week, you are going to start to let go of some of

your withheld anger. As you do, you will be freeing your mind and body to enjoy more sexual pleasure. There are several ways to go about this. You may choose the one best suited to you or try all of them.

The first is to sit down for five minutes each day and make a list of all the things that made you angry that day. Start each item on the list with "Today I am angry about _____."

Then spend another five minutes trying to remember whatever past angers you are holding on to, and fill in the sentence "I am still angry about _____." This is one way to begin to release the anger. It gets it off your chest and onto paper.

The second method for releasing anger is to get yourself a box of crayons and some drawing paper. Now sit down and use colors to express how you feel inside. You may draw realistic pictures that convey your feelings or just scribble your anger out onto the page with strokes of the crayon.

For the third method, find a fairly soundproof room in your house. Put a large pillow in front of you and bang your fists into it, yelling "I'm angry at _____." If you are afraid of the neighbors, just try screaming into a pillow.

The fourth solution is to muster the courage to tell someone you are angry with him or her. This doesn't mean you need to open the issue for discussion. Tell the person why you are angry, hear the reply, and try to forgive him or her and let go of your angry feelings. This is particularly important to do if you are holding on to anger toward your sexual partner.

Remember, anger and love are very bad bedfellows. If you want to improve your capacity for love and sexual enjoyment, you need to release some of that withheld anger. One or more of these techniques can start you on your way toward tearing down some of the walls you've built up to keep anger in, which in the end only serve to keep pleasure out.

I create a good atmosphere for lovemaking.

You have your partner, you've found a place where you can be alone, and you have set aside the time. What is the next step in assuring a satisfying sexual experience? Can you remember a time when everything was ready for take-off—except that the bed linens seemed soiled? Or perhaps the room needed a good cleaning? Creating an atmosphere where you feel comfortable, relaxed, and in the mood is a very important ingredient for making love.

You can create an atmosphere that is romantic, sexual, or sensual. The atmosphere can be whatever you wish to create, but it takes a conscious act to make the physical environment mirror your mood.

Take the time this week to look around your "living space." Do you feel comfortable in it? As you look around, think about what it would be like if you were seeing it for the first time. Is it clean? Are the lights too bright or dim?

What can you add or take away that might help you create the atmosphere you desire?

Freshly cut flowers are always a good way to set the mood. A just-picked bouquet of wildflowers will give the room a welcome, homey appearance, while exotic blooms set an exciting scene. Candles create a soft glow. Music is also a mood inducer. Jazz, classical—the choice is yours. An open bottle of wine or brandy next to two glasses can set the stage for romance. Oils and massage lotions on a tray atop a night table suggest the possibility of an evening of touching and tenderness. Don't forget your sense of touch—soft cotton sheets or warm wool blankets can make your bed even more inviting.

Placing a mirror in an advantageous position often can add another dimension to the sexual experience and help to create an air of freedom and exploration.

This week, become more aware of your private space for you and your partner. Allow your imagination to run free and help you create an atmosphere to enhance your sexual experience.

I will do the things I've never done before.

Many of us have set beliefs about the way we should be. This list usually includes the way we should behave sexually, what we should and should not do, what we should and should not like. These "shoulds" come from our parents, our teachers, TV, and magazines. The problem with the list is that it keeps us bound, tied up, and usually bored in our sexual explorations.

How do we let go of the list? This week, take time alone to write a list of all the things you have never done sexually. Explore every aspect of your sexual experience. Do not judge yourself, and do not limit yourself by the belief that good girls or good boys don't do these things. Have fun. Perhaps you have never taken a bath together or made love on the beach. Maybe there's a position that you have never tried, or maybe you would never have thought of using a vibrator. Just keep adding to your list. Remember all the scenes in the movies that may have excited you.

What about those scenes in books that turned you on? Keep adding to this list all week.

At the end of the week, after you have compiled a list of things that you never have done sexually, review your list. Take time and see what one thing on this list you would most like to try. Choose something that you would feel comfortable doing with your partner. Your partner should also have one new exciting idea and experience that she or he wants to share with you. If you are not in a relationship, choose something you can do alone or something you would feel safe doing with a new or casual lover. Maybe it's a new way of masturbating or dressing up in sexy clothes in the privacy of your bedroom. If you are sleeping with a new lover, you could try being more or less sexually aggressive, depending on your norm.

If you are feeling daring and want to add even more spice to your sexual experience, choose one of the items on your list that is a little more risky. But be sure you feel safe with both your environment and any other people involved. While this is a time to experiment and expand your sexual repertoire, it is not a time to throw caution to the wind. By trying some of the things on your list and experiencing something new, you will add another dimension to your sex life. If you are in a long-term relationship, it will give it a new beginning. If you are single, it will open up new sexual possibilities. The choice is yours.

I set aside enough time for sexual pleasure.

☐

Setting aside enough time to make love is this week's thought. Because of the busy lives we live, our sexual needs usually do not take precedence in the planning of our days. Even if we think about sex throughout the day, we often don't schedule a time for sexual sharing.

If you want more from your sexual encounters than you are receiving, perhaps you are not giving sex priority in your life. Do you take responsibility for setting aside enough time for making love? Is this a conscious thought? Do you include it in your schedule? Or do you just believe that it will fall into place and just take care of itself?

This week, take time to schedule sex into your life. Start by looking at the week ahead. It may be helpful to write out your schedule. Include your work, chores, and time with your children. Now notice where there is some free time: a time when the kids are away or asleep, a time when work and chores are done, a time you may have ordinarily used to watch TV or chat on the phone. Take that time and write sex into your schedule. If your schedule is so tight that you can't find any free time, you will need to drop some activity and replace it with time for sex.

At least once this week, set aside a special time to make love. Once you have given yourself this time, don't let anything interfere. This week, your commitment to your sex life is to be given the same or greater importance than any of your other activities. This means making sure you will not be interrupted. Take phones off the hook; leave your business at the office and your worries outside the bedroom door.

This is your time for pleasure. Realize that you are giving yourself a precious gift—the time to love your partner slowly and completely. Be sure to use the entire time you have set aside. You may have enough time to bathe together before making love or to share a sensual dinner afterward. But most important, allow yourself to linger in these special moments you have given yourself. Once you try this, you probably will want to include sex in your schedule a lot more often.

Deep breathing enhances sexual pleasure.

Learning to breathe deeply is one of the simplest, most effective techniques you can use to increase your sexual pleasure. It is instinctual for human beings to hold their breath when they want to avoid feeling something. For example, a person who is frightened will stop breathing momentarily or make her breaths quite shallow in order not to feel overwhelmed by fear. We have all done this so often in our lives that by the time we are adults, holding our breath has become a habit. We live with a less than sufficient supply of oxygen, which serves to keep our feelings subdued. It also diminishes the flow of vital life energy through our bodies. How can we expect to enjoy sex, to reach the pinnacles of pleasure, if we deaden our feelings by not breathing?

Because we are so conditioned to shallow breathing, it is helpful to practice the following deep breathing technique, not only to prepare us for lovemaking, but to enhance the quality of our lives in general.

Lie down on your back and become as comfortable as possible. Loosen any clothing that is tight or binding. First, notice your natural breathing. Can you feel yourself breathing? Can you hear yourself? Does your body expand and contract? Place a hand on your chest. Do you feel movement? Now place a hand on your belly. Is it moving in response to your breath? Now begin to breathe gently through your mouth. Concentrate on your exhalation, pushing out as much air as possible. Then simply allow yourself to fill up with air again as you inhale. Do this a few times until you feel a natural rhythm developing. Allow your inhalations and exhalations to form a circle, and relax into an organic rhythm of taking in and letting go. Try to keep your mind quiet as you focus on your breath. You probably will begin to feel relaxed and refreshed.

Now that you know how to breathe deeply, remember to do so the next time you make love. Notice how much more alive it makes you feel. If you have been keeping your breathing shallow for a long time, you may experience some fear as your feelings increase in intensity. Just breathe through the fear. Try breathing through your mouth, even emitting sounds—this is particularly important during orgasm. Just remember, the more you breathe, the more you fire your sexual feelings to reach a peak and spill over into a fully satisfying release.

Massage can be a doorway to a heightened sexual experience.

☐

When most people think of massage, they think of relaxation and unwinding. This week, you'll have the opportunity to explore a whole new aspect of massage—the release of tension from key areas of the body to promote a greater flow of sexual energy.

The more open your body is, the greater its potential for sexual pleasure. When you hold tension in any part of your body, you have decreased feeling in that area. Since sex is all about increased feeling, tension puts a damper on the experience.

There are several areas of the body that are considered key tension spots. These include the top of the head, the base of the skull, the neck and shoulders, and the lower legs and ankles. If these areas are freed of tension, you'll find your sexual excitement can soar.

You'll give yourself a great gift this week if you set time aside to exchange twenty minutes of massage before foreplay begins. This should be a time devoted to deeply massaging those key tension spots. It is fine to make this massage sensual, as long as you keep your focus on deep muscle relaxation rather than tickling.

As you massage, really get your hands into all those tense muscles—massage, stroke firmly, and knead. Go as deeply as your partner can tolerate—and remember to breathe. If you don't breathe, it's like holding on while you're trying to let go—you just sabotage your effort.

Massaging each other while you are making love can also be a wonderful experience. It releases all the energy that has become jammed up at tension points, letting it flow through your entire body, bringing aliveness, pleasure, to every inch of you—not just your genitals. As the tension is released, your partner will feel the heightened energy flow as well. This in turn will cause your partner to become more excited, until you are passing your passion back and forth with greater and greater intensity. The more intensity you build, the greater your pleasure. A massage and the release of energy in the muscles can bring you a great deal of sexual satisfaction.

Remember, sex should be a full-body experience, with exciting vibrations from head to toe. Try some deep massage this week. It will bring you to a heightened awareness of your body and your lover's as well.

Orgasm can be a peak experience for me.

[ ]

Orgasm can provide us with the opportunity to have a peak experience. What does it mean to have a peak experience? It means that for a brief time we expand beyond the limits of our individual ego. It is a moment of oneness in which we do not feel a separation between us and the world. It is a surrender that brings with it a sense of awe, delight, or wonder. It is generally accompanied by extremely pleasurable feelings streaming through our bodies. Such peak experiences can be attained through religious rituals when a person feels at one with God. Or they can be found looking at a sunset or naturescape and feeling at one with the universe. The birth of a baby or the discovery of a long-sought-after solution to a problem can initiate a peak experience. And orgasm, by its very definition, has the power to move us to the same heights. This is why you might have heard it referred to as "holy." In fact, there are many religions that see sex, when properly channeled, as a path to God.

Orgasm is defined as "the climax of sexual excitement." It comes from the Greek word *orgasmos*, which means to be lustful, to swell. Freud has written that the orgasm results from the buildup of tension in the genitals. In his book *Love and Orgasm*, Wilhelm Reich describes this process as the surrender of the entire body to the involuntary process. The French have called it *le petit mort*, or the little death, because it can be experienced as a total loss of control.

In this relinquishing of rational control, this surrender to the body's involuntary pulsations, is the capacity for a spiritual or transcendent experience. As the mind detaches and empties, we can begin to let go of our separate ego identities, releasing us into a stream of expanded consciousness. We feel momentarily at one with our mates and the world. We are washed in a primal sea of pleasure and sensuality.

Although we all have the capacity for orgasm to be a peak experience, it is usually a rare occurrence. This is true because, simply put, we are afraid on one level or another to surrender so fully. We fear being that out of control. For some, this fear prevents orgasm altogether; for others it greatly diminishes the experience. This, by the way, goes for men as well as women. Just because a man ejaculates does not mean he is having a full orgasm.

This week, think about your orgasms. Are you able to have them? Have you ever had one that was a peak experience? If not, imagine what it would be like to experience orgasm so intensely. Then think about what stops you from doing so.

Once you have done this, simply know what is possible for you as a human being. Don't use this knowledge to chastise yourself or feel inadequate. That's not the point. Just know that peak-experience orgasms are possible and that with self-love, trust, and a little practice you may eventually be able to experience the joy of surrendering to one.

I luxuriate in the afterglow of sex.

After orgasm, partners begin to separate, both physically and emotionally. This stage, called the *afterglow*, is as important as foreplay.

Take some time now to remember how you feel after orgasm. Do you feel absolutely satisfied? Do you feel as if you are airborne? Do you feel tired? Do you feel energized? Do you want to talk? Do you feel disconnected, separate, and lonely? Do you like to just relax and be silent? It may be different at different times.

Going through your past experiences will be very helpful, particularly if you are able to keep a record of your feelings about these memories. For example, after each remembrance, answer this question:

After my orgasm I feel _____.

Keep a running list, and review your responses periodically. Do you see a pattern emerging?

Now that you have recognized your particular response to the postorgasmic state, try an experiment. If we rush away after orgasm, we actually prevent ourselves from experiencing one of the integral stages of the human sexual experience. This week, we will focus on luxuriating in the afterglow of sex. Give yourself at least ten minutes to experience yourself and your partner after having sex. If you have no lover this week, take the time after masturbating to think about how you feel. If you usually rush off to take a shower after sex, have a towel or maybe some warm water and a washcloth close by and make cleanup a part of afterglow. You may want to be silent or to touch each other gently. Perhaps you need to share some feelings or even drift off to sleep. If you are alone, take the time to enjoy your body, or allow your mind to drift peacefully. See what emerges. Whatever you do, it's important to honor the resolution stage of sex. It can be extremely relaxing and can become a pleasurable part of sex you won't want to miss.

There are many ways
to reach orgasm.

□

We are often concerned about our sex lives getting boring and unexciting. One way to spice things up is to free ourselves from the belief that sex always means intercourse. This week, let's explore some alternatives.

What are the ways you can come to orgasm without intercourse? Give yourself some time to explore gently whatever options you can come up with. What we are seeking is a variety of ways to make lovemaking more enjoyable.

Consider trying some of the following techniques. The first is masturbation. Manually manipulating your partner to orgasm can be fun. This can be used for making love when one partner does not want to be aroused but still wants to give pleasure to the other. It can also be used when one partner has reached a climax before the other but still wants to give pleasure to the other. Mutually masturbating can not only be an erotic experience but it can teach you your partner's rhythm and what really works for her.

Does she like to be stimulated slowly or quickly—does she prefer a light touch or a heavy hand?

Oral stimulation, "sixty-nine," fellatio, and cunnilingus, are different words for the same experience. This is using the tongue and the mouth to stimulate the genitals. Some people find this a highly pleasurable sexual experience and a satisfying way to reach orgasm. If you find this offensive, do not judge yourself, but do try to put aside your judgments of anyone who does enjoy this form of sexual exploration.

Do not forget—the vibrator can be a great aid in making lovemaking without intercourse exciting. It is a wonderful toy in the sexual repertoire.

Lovemaking without intercourse is a creative option when birth control is unavailable. It is also useful if one of the partners happens to be incapacitated because of illness or injury—for example, when one partner has a bad back or a broken limb.

No matter what the situation, opening your mind to varied techniques means opening your sexual life to new and exciting possibilities. Sex without intercourse can be lots of fun. Try it and see.

There's more to sex than orgasm.

□

It might be a great relief to many to realize that there is more to sex than orgasm. Striving and reaching to achieve orgasm can become compulsive and can rob you of a fulfilling sexual experience. The self-imposed pressure to perform and to have a "knock-your-socks-off" orgasm can create sexual problems. This is directly related to the fact that orgasm is an experience of surrender and letting go. The more we are able to let go of our rational minds, the more we can give over to the streaming, spontaneous, muscular pulsations of an orgasm. If we are busy worrying whether we'll have an orgasm or if it will be a "good" one, we are identified with our controlling mind. And if we are in control, how can we let go? We suddenly find ourselves in a vicious cycle of worrying about orgasms so much that we lose the capacity to surrender to one. This causes us to become even more obsessive, finally leaving us frustrated and depressed.

The key to breaking this vicious cycle is to take the pressure off.

For many, the destination has been more important than the journey. If this has been true for you, you may be missing a lot of pleasure. Consider the possibility of exploring each other's bodies, of gently touching and passionately playing, of talking, of laughing, of growing closer, and of snuggling intimately—of savoring small sensations and nurturing your more subtle feelings. Take some time now to check out how you would feel if you could let go of orgasm as the necessary outcome of a sexual experience. Then try having a sexual experience this week where orgasm is not your goal. If you have an orgasm, great, but don't try to force it. Just enjoy and explore all the feelings you are having. Delight in each moment instead of blindly rushing to the climax. You should be infinitely more satisfied by this experience, and it will lay the groundwork for you to surrender to more satisfying orgasms in the future.

Letting go of false myths about orgasm may bring me greater pleasure.

☐

Most of us were raised with myths about sex that continue to influence us today. One such myth has been told to countless little boys—that if they masturbate, their penises will fall off. Another is the scare story that a woman can lock a man's penis inside her vagina with her muscles alone.

Myths about orgasm seem the most plentiful and the most varied. Here is just a sampling of the myths—and the realities:

1. If you really had a great sex life, and if you loved each other, you would have simultaneous orgasms. You would "come" together.

The truth is that reaching orgasm together is not a common or natural experience for most couples. It is something that can be worked toward in a gentle way, but if it is rigidly upheld as an ideal, it only creates unnecessary frustration and dissatisfaction.

2. There is an immaturity in women who do not
    have vaginal orgasms.

The reality is that very few women experience vaginal orgasm. To experience any orgasm, the source of the orgasm, the clitoris, must be stimulated. A belief in this myth might prevent a woman from feeling free to explore alternative ways to reach orgasm. On the other hand, it will lead many a man to feel inadequate because he falsely believes he can't satisfy his woman.

3. If a man does not have an orgasm, he will suffer
    great pain, called "blue balls."

It is important to note that it is no more painful for a man not to reach orgasm than it is for a woman.

4. The only mature way to reach orgasm is through
    coitus, that is, intercourse.

In actuality, the only "mature" way to reach orgasm is to allow yourself permission to have one any way you are able. To believe in this myth would surely limit your capacity for sexual exploration and fun.

5. It is not good to have orgasm while
    menstruating.

It is a medical fact that the contractions experienced during orgasm when menstruating relieve the menstrual cramps. Some women also find that they are at the height of sexuality during menstruation.

6. Orgasm during pregnancy is not good for the mother-to-be.

There is a belief that the contractions might set off labor, so it is advised at the end of gestation that there be no intercourse, but it has been reported by pregnant women that they are very orgasmic during pregnancy because of the additional hormones.

Perhaps some of your myths about orgasm match those listed here. Work on letting go of some of these false beliefs and liberate yourself from the constrictions they may have imposed on your sex life.

I choose to follow my positive sexual teachings.

☐

How did you learn about sex? Most young children learn about sex from their parents, relatives, and friends. Who we become sexually is a tapestry woven by the lessons we learn from these people: from their overt teachings and their more subtle sexual behavior and attitudes, we formed our sexual identities. These teachings usually include both positive and negative aspects. In order to live happy and fulfilled sexual lives, we need to honor and live by the positive things we were taught. More important, we must recognize and change the teachings we have incorporated that limit our sexual pleasure and freedom.

This week, we will focus on an exploration of our sexual teachers—both positive and negative. Let's start with the most influential sexual models in your life, your parents. Were they positive or negative teachers, or a combination of both? By thinking about the following questions, you may get a clearer sense of what they felt about sex and how they communicated that to you.

Do you remember asking questions about where babies

come from? Were your questions answered calmly and without embarrassment, or were they ignored or made fun of? Perhaps your questions were answered with evasions. Can you see how this might have led you to believe that sex is something to be ashamed of?

Perhaps you witnessed your mother getting undressed or saw your father naked. What were their responses? Do you remember what you felt? Did you feel as if you had done something bad? Were you made to feel naughty? If so, this might affect how you feel about your body and nudity today.

Now take a moment to fill in the blanks.

My father believed sex was
_____.

My mother believed sex was
_____.

Try to sense the attitudes they communicated to you either by their words or behavior. Were they secretive about sex? Did you ever see them kissing or hugging? Did they reprimand you for masturbating? Did they emanate shame or openness about sex? Did they tell you about sex, or were you left to find out in some other way?

Now follow the string from their attitudes to your judgments and assumptions about sex. For example, if your parents never showed affection in front of you, you may feel on some level that showing affection publicly is distasteful. On the positive side, if your parents taught you about sex without embarrassment, you probably are more comfortable with your sexuality today.

Now think about some of your other sexual teachers. First look at those who fostered negative feelings about sex. Did another child give you frightening or false sexual information? Did a relative or baby-sitter ever reprimand you for masturbating or warn you of the wiles of the opposite sex? Was an early lover cruel or humiliating? Perhaps your negative teaching was a rigid religious upbringing, which caused you to feel sex was "dirty." Again, draw connections between your negative teachers and the inhibitions you may feel today.

Now remember your positive sexual teachers. They may include your parents, a lover who inititated you to the joys of sex, or a psychotherapist who helped you realize that sex is a normal and enjoyable part of life. It may have been a sex-education teacher or even a book that gave you permission to explore the full scope of your sexuality.

Finally, decide this week to say good-bye to your negative teachers. Tell them you no longer want to be influenced by them, and imagine yourself turning your back and walking away. Then imagine yourself walking toward your positive sexual teachers. Thank them for all they've given you, and commit yourself to living by the lessons they've taught you. Remember you are an adult now and can freely choose your mentors. Choose the ones who exemplify freedom and life-affirming sexual attitudes.

I don't take my mind to bed.

Imagine the most perfectly romantic, sexually stimulating, visually arousing scene. Allow the details to move into focus. This time everything is exactly the way you dreamed. You are in each other's arms, but just as you are ready to let go, a thought comes into your mind. Your body stiffens, and the ability to let go is gone. Thoughts of business, the children, and the outside move in, and now it is no longer the two of you. You have taken your mind to bed with you, and the room has become very crowded.

You are no longer in the moment with your partner. The result is a dulled sexual experience. There are many reasons for taking your mind to bed with you. The most obvious is an inability to let go of the cares and concerns of your daily life. Things that are unfinished or unsettled seem to pop up like targets in a shooting gallery, drawing your attraction first here, then there. Sometimes your mind becomes busy planning tomorrow's chores or Saturday night's party menu. Other times you may be worrying about how your body looks or how you are performing. Still another common mind game is worrying about whether you will have an orgasm.

Whatever the subject matter, when you allow your mind to interfere with your sexual experience, it is usually because you want to avoid being fully involved and fully present. This may have to do with a fear of sexual intensity or a fear of facing some feelings you may be trying to hide. Instead of taking responsibility for your feelings so that you can make changes, you let your mind wander.

This week, practice not taking your mind to bed. One tool you may find helpful is to clear your mind before you begin making love. Transcribe the lists you're carrying around in your head onto paper. Share your fears or anger, shame or insecurity, with your mate. If that's too difficult, write them out and then forget them for the next half hour. You can always continue thinking about them later.

If you find your mind wandering during lovemaking, don't give in to it. This takes some discipline, but it puts you in control. When thoughts begin to invade, simply say "later" to them and concentrate on your lover's body or on your own feelings.

If you begin to feel angry or frightened by this process, just note it, and know that you have something to contemplate after your lovemaking has ended.

For the most part, taking your mind to bed is just a bad habit. With a little discipline and self-control, you can learn how to give sex your full attention. When you do, you enhance your potential for feeling wonderful and joyful. Next time, don't take your mind to bed. Have a full-bodied experience instead.

Mutual trust allows for greater surrender.

☐

While you may like a little danger at times and find it fans your sexual fires, the fact is that in order to have truly fulfilling sexual experiences you need to trust both your mate and yourself.

Sex is one of the greatest acts of surrender human beings can participate in. It is on this level of surrender that sex has been likened to a spiritual experience. During orgasm, the ego releases its tightly held control, and the body and mind give over to strong involuntary pulsations. The more you release, the more pleasure you enjoy.

Although you may have had moments when it was easy to surrender sexually to a stranger, for the most part we need to trust the person we are with in order to let go sexually with them. In fact, deciding to become involved sexually with someone we don't trust is not only stupid—it can be downright dangerous. This is not to say that a one-night stand can't be fun—you just need to pay careful attention to your intuition. Can this person be trusted with your body? In such a case, you must trust yourself, knowing how much you can let go and when to bring things to an end.

But in the long run, the deepest sexual pleasure you can attain comes when you trust your lover deeply. Here is a person who will see you without restraint—naked and writhing, screaming with intense pleasure—shivering with the release of your ego boundaries. Here is a person with whom you can share your sexual fantasies, your desires, your likes and dislikes.

And just because a couple has been together for a long time does not immediately insure mutual trust. Trust is something that must be nurtured and developed.

This week, begin to create an atmosphere of mutual trust with your sexual partner or lover. It may help simply to share your fears of letting go with each other. Tell each other where and when you feel embarrassed or shy. Maybe you are too self-conscious to yell when having an orgasm. Or perhaps you feel uncomfortable being as aggressively passionate as you'd like to be. Receive each other's assurances that you will be accepted, no matter how you look, act, or sound. Then, the next time you make love, actively trust your partner with your sexuality. Let go. Do whatever it is you had been afraid to do. Be as passionate or loud as you want to be. Remember, it is mutual trust that sets the stage for complete surrender.

The greatest lover is the person who loves himself.

☐

Everyone asks: What makes a good lover? Are there techniques? Is there some acquired knowledge that can help to teach a person to be an excellent lover? The answer is yes; yet even if you learned all the techniques, you still may not be the best lover. You may have learned how to please, and even tease, but the greatest lover is the person who has learned to love himself.

This might surprise you, but it is true. The person who has learned to take care of his own needs, who has learned to accept himself as he is in the moment, who has learned not to seek approval outside of himself, who has learned that he is not meant to live up to another's expectations, is the person who has learned to support and nurture himself. In this act of self-loving, he has learned not to deny his feelings, his needs, and indeed, his sexuality. Our sexual behavior is a mirror of our psychological development. The person who loves himself can then truly open his heart to another.

When we are unsure of ourselves, when we feel we are not good enough, we usually seek validation from another source. We look for praise, for agreement, outside of ourselves. We are tense and self-conscious. Our sexuality becomes a statement of our inhibitions and our negative feelings.

Take the time this week, each day, to see where you have been unloving to yourself. To love yourself, you must accept all your feelings and all your failings. Gently observe yourself. Ask yourself these questions: "How wasn't I loving to myself today? Where didn't I accept how I was feeling? Where didn't I listen to my intuition, and denied my inner voice?" Go over this scenario very gently. See if there was a time where you might have said yes when you wanted to say no or said no when you wanted to say yes. Self-loving is seeing yourself, giving to yourself, and accepting yourself.

The self-lover has opened his heart to himself, to all of his feelings, and these include his fear, his anger, his rage, his joy, his passion. He knows that each feeling is another color in his emotional rainbow. He accepts himself. When he makes love with another, it is with a sense of joy, and trust. His heart is opened to himself and therefore can open to his lover. When you love yourself, you know that you are the gift. In giving this gift, you have surrendered, and it is this act of surrender that makes you the greatest lover you can possibly be.

Giving to my lover is giving to me.

So far, we have been concerning ourselves with how to enhance our own sexual pleasure. This week we will turn the tables and concentrate on how we can be better lovers. More specifically, we will forgo seeking after our own enjoyment and instead find ways to give pleasure to our mates and lovers. You'll be surprised how focusing on someone other than yourself can free up your sexual energy and actually give you great pleasure.

The first step is to know what your lover likes. If you haven't actually asked her recently, do so. Encourage her to tell all, and assure her that you can be trusted with her erotic fantasies and desires. Get her to be specific. Does she like her toes sucked or her neck nibbled? Would a whipped cream party turn her on? How about a champagne bath?

Next, pick a few things she has mentioned—things you are comfortable with and feel you'd enjoy giving her—and then go ahead. Pleasure her. Don't be afraid to ask questions as you proceed. "Is this the way you like it? Is it better if I move this way?" Give it your all. Tonight you are the world's greatest lover, pleasing your mate. Let go of any thoughts of what you want in return.

Experiment with allowing yourself to be turned on by your giving—by the knowledge that you are sexy and are turning on your partner. If you really let go and provide as much pleasure as you can for your lover, you'll find the old adage "It is better to give than to receive" to be gloriously true. Not only will you receive love, gratitude, and appreciation in return for your efforts, your lover will probably be so aroused that she will return the attention with the same sexual intensity.

Remember, sexual energy is a real and palpable thing. If you turn your partner on, the raw energy of her sexual excitement will be communicated to you, turning you on to turn her on even more—it's a delicious pleasure circle.

Put yourself aside this week. Attend to your lover, and feel the power, fun, and joy of giving.

I can have kinky sex without guilt.

Kinky sex without guilt. Is that possible? What indeed is kinky sex? *Kinky* is anything you judge to be out of the norm. What is kinky for some is definitely not kinky for others. *Kinky* ends up being a matter of judgment. This week's thought can help you give up your judgments and guilt about kinky sex and even stimulate you into trying some.

Take a few minutes to think about what you regard as sexually kinky. Allow your mind to visualize and fantasize. Play and have fun. Do not hold yourself back by being concerned about what someone else might think. For now, forget about everyone "out there."

What do you regard as kinky? Let's play. Do you imagine yourself getting dressed up in clothing of the opposite sex? Try it. How does it feel? Do you like wearing high heels and outrageously sexy garter belts and really "strutting your stuff"? Now buy yourself the sexiest garter belt you can find. Take the kinky sex as far as you can. Have fun exploring new ways of being or parts of you that you've never expressed.

What can be fun and also add new excitement to an ongoing relationship is to explore your "kinky" fantasies with your partner. It can be a turn-on to share. What is a wonderful treat is when your partner's kinky sex fantasies match yours. If you think you'd like to tie someone up, how wonderful it would be if your partner says he might enjoy being tied up. Sharing fantasies and playing them out with a willing partner can be another ingredient in your sexual banquet. Remember, kinky sex without guilt can be fun.

Cleanliness can enhance sexual pleasure.

Have you ever been in this situation? You are alone at last. The lights are low, the music soft and romantic. This is the moment you have been waiting for all week. Suddenly, instead of romance, the only thing on your mind is that your deodorant has worn off and that your breath is stale. You feel self-conscious and uncomfortable.

Another scenario may be that you have the perfect person in your arms. There is nothing about this person you do not like except a faint musky odor. Our body scents may be natural, but what do you do when someone's scent turns you off?

It is a taboo in our culture to comment on our own or another's hygiene; yet not mentioning it can destroy a relationship even before it begins. We let our embarrassment shame us into silence instead of taking the situation in hand. It's not necessary to be rudely explicit, but a gentle suggestion for a mutual shower or a request to freshen up before lovemaking can make the difference between a night of fun and surrender and one of judgments and inhibitions.

This goes for your surroundings as well. Clean sheets feel great on naked bodies.

This week, enjoy some squeaky-clean sex.

Sex can be a dance.

Sex can be a dance. Sex can be fun. Sex can be spontaneous. Sex can be primitive. Sex is being in your body and enjoying your body. Sex is about being playful and having fun.

Now invite your partner to bed with you. You can even do this exercise on the floor. Lie side by side with your partner. When the music starts, begin to move a part of your body. Respond to the music; let the music move you. Feel it; just let it happen. Be the music. As your body starts moving, allow it to connect with some part of your partner's body. Invite your partner to dance with you. Start slowly. Let your arms or legs start moving together. Let every part of the two of you make contact. Feel the movement becoming a part of you; feel the passion moving you. Allow all parts of you to dance, to feel the intensity of the music and of your contact with each other. Let the music guide you: follow its pulse until you are vibrating together. Don't worry about whether you consummate this dance—

if it happens, great; if it doesn't happen, that's okay, too. The point is to lose yourself in your physicality—allow the music to help you let go of your mind and get fully into your body. Dance; have fun; celebrate the joy of movement. When the music is over, you may even want to ask your partner for another dance.

Enjoy the dance of sex. Feel the energy between you.

Water meditation can increase sexual pleasure.

To truly enjoy sex, you must be able to enjoy your sensuality. Sensuality refers to the pleasures of the senses. Since sex as a total experience involves each of our five senses, heightening our awareness in each of them will improve our capacity for sexual pleasure.

This week, you are being given a very pleasurable exercise, which will help you to let go and explore your sexual self. This exercise can be done alone or with a partner. It will bring you into a space of deep relaxation and loving. It creates a womblike atmosphere, a tranquillity tank for you that can also be an experience of shared bliss with your partner.

Light your bathroom by candle. You can place the candles around the rim of the tub. You may also place them on the floor of the bathroom. Have your favorite tape ready. If you are doing this exercise alone, step into the tub, which you have filled with warm water. Submerge yourself as completely as possible, and let yourself float and relax.

113

Allow yourself to take in all the smells, sights, and sounds of this special sensual environment you have entered. Give in fully to sensual meditation. If you are with a partner, undress her very gently, and allow her to undress you. Fill your bath with warm water, adding lightly scented bath oil or salts.

Now step into the tub together. One of you places your back against the tub. Allow your partner to lie between your legs, as much of her submerged as possible, except her face. Take a few minutes to get comfortable. The person in back may gently place his hands on his partner's heart and feel the gentle beating. Allow yourselves just to "float," experiencing the water, the light, and the calmness. Feel the water gently caressing your body. Let all five of your senses become aware of this experience. Feel your partner's body against you own. Smell the subtle scents the oils have created. Listen to the sounds of the water, of your own breath, of your partner's heart beating. Take in the visual beauty of the candles and the shadows they cast. Luxuriate in each sensual moment.

When you are ready, after about five minutes, or more, if you like, at a prearranged nonverbal signal, switch positions. Let yourself go; feel your body floating; feel yourself surrounded by your lover. Feel the nurturing of this moment; feel your wholeness. This water meditation can be a prelude to a wonderful night of sex.

I ask for what I like
and say what I don't
like.

Asking for what you like is an important step in creating your sexual pleasure. It is taking responsibility for sharing with your partner what feels good. It takes into consideration that your partner may not know what you like, and that he cannot guess. Asking for what you want is the first step toward getting it.

Saying what you don't like is equally important. Don't just feel angry, invaded, or bored. Share with your partner; help her to know what your body enjoys and what your mind and body rejects. Taking responsibility for saying what you don't like will add a sense of freedom to your sexual encounters.

Many of us have trouble discussing our sexual desires and making requests of our partners. The roots of these problems may have been planted in childhood. Perhaps you were taught that it was impolite to ask for something that you wanted or that you would be thought greedy or demanding. Perhaps you were taught that if you told someone that you didn't like something, you would hurt their feelings, and they might not like you anymore. These beliefs influence our sexual behavior and keep you from having as much pleasure as you might.

This week, gently observe yourself while you are making love. Become aware of one thing you would like your partner to do for you; then find the courage to ask for it. It may be a new way of being kissed or a new erogenous area of your body waiting to be caressed.

At another time, tell your partner the things you do not like. For example, perhaps you never liked the way he licked your ears but always felt too afraid to mention it. By asking for what you like and saying what you don't like, you will keep your relationship alive and well. You will learn how to give each other the greatest possible pleasure, while at the same time, decrease frustration, boredom, resentment, and guilt that build up because you don't fulfill your desires.

Take responsibility for yourself as a sexual being this week. Ask for what you like; say what you don't like. Then just lie back and enjoy the rewards of sexual adulthood.

Keeping the excitement in my long-term relationship.

Anything new is mysterious, exciting, and challenging. Entering a sexual relationship causes the heart to beat faster and the adrenaline to flow. Falling in love is an adventure of getting to know another person and allowing her or him to get to know you.

Most lovers say they will never let their relationship become ordinary, mundane, or boring. They promise that their relationship will be different. Yet, more often than not, the promise that they had such good intentions of keeping somehow gets lost. They forget the good intentions and take the path of least resistance. It begins to appear as if there is nothing new to learn about the other person and that their once-passionate sexual relationship is now nothing more than a comfortable exchange.

Take some time to remember what it was like at the beginning of your relationship. Recall the excitement, the passion, and the desire that you felt for each other. Then plan an evening with no interruptions—perhaps a dinner out, where you can share these memories and anecdotes with each other. Allow the memories to rekindle your desire. This will be the first step in knowing that sex in a long-term relationship can be a deepening and enriching experience. Begin to share your longings and your secret wish for more. In this opening of your hearts to each other is the seed of the renewal of your passion.

The potential for the deepest sexual experience you can ever have rests in your long-term relationship. When two people have been together for many years, they develop a mutual trust that can allow them to unite very deeply in a strong sexual bond. The trust can form the bedrock for wide experimentation, wild passion, and ecstatic surrender. With such possibilities before us, it is a shame that we often neglect to put in the required effort. In a new relationship, we are carried by our passion; in a long-term relationship, we must nurture, protect, and feed our passion. A long-term relationship demands more self-responsibility, depends more on tenderness, and requires more giving, but the rewards are well worth it.

This week, realize how precious your long-term relationship is and make a commitment to keep its sexuality alive. Decide to make the effort—you will receive great pleasure and delight in return.

I will not follow habits that limit my sexuality.

□

How we think and what we think can limit our experiences. Everything we believe either limits our growth or allows for unbounded creativity. This is particularly true of our sex life—acting habitually lessens our capacity for joy, pleasure, and fulfillment.

When you behave unconsciously, you are unaware of your behavior and are acting out of habit. Acting out of habit leads you to believe that you have no choices, which can lead you to behavior that is mechanical, routinized, and most probably, boring.

This week, observe your unconscious and habitual behavior. Do this gently, without vengeance. Its reward will be added spontaneity and diversity in your sexual life.

To begin, imagine you and your lover lying in bed. Do you always make love in bed? Have you ever thought of making love on the sofa, on the floor, or in the bathtub? When do you make love? Some people get into the habit of making love after they shower, after they brush their teeth, after the eleven-o'clock news. Can you see how that might destroy the possibility for spontaneous passion? Have you ever thought about making love before dinner? Do you see the possibilities?

Take your time and explore how acting habitually limits your sexuality. Then do something to change the situation. If you are always passive, try being the aggressor. If you are always aggressive, allow yourself to discover the pleasures of being the passive partner. If you usually make love in the same position, try a new one. There are so many options to choose from—have fun and explore the possibilities.

This week, discover at least one area of your sex life in which you act habitually, and replace it with something new and spontaneous. You may find it fun and exciting.

I reclaim my sexual innocence.

Childhood is a time of sexual innocence. A child discovers through self-exploration that certain sensations feel good. When children become interested in the uniqueness of their bodies, they begin to ask questions about their bodies and notice how different their parents' bodies are. They also begin to explore one another's bodies.

This should be a wonderful and exciting time. However, as children, many of us grew up in an atmosphere of sexual repression. Our natural curiosity was forced underground. We were made to feel guilty about the new pleasures we felt. Sex became something bad and forbidden.

Though our innocence may have been betrayed when we were children, there is no reason we cannot reclaim it today.

To have a sense of innocence about your sexuality will enable you to feel new and fresh about your experiences. It can free your curiosity to explore new areas of sexuality as a child would—with excitement and eagerness. It can reawaken your curiosity without the fear of someone implying that your interests are perverse.

This week, become a child again. Put aside your inhibitions. Try to remember how you felt about your sexuality before anyone interfered. If you can't remember, just imagine what it must have been like. Then go ahead and engage in some sexual activity with a childlike innocence. Try exploring your body as if you were discovering it for the first time. Or try exploring your partner's body as if you had never seen a member of the opposite sex. Play doctor. Satisfy your curiosity by following it wherever it leads you. There is no one to stop you. Be playful; have fun.

Return to innocence and regain the freedom to enjoy one of life's greatest pleasures: your unrepressed, natural, and guilt-free sexuality.

Taking precautions
takes the worry
out of sex.

□

It is difficult to feel free and open sexually if you are worrying about the consequences of your encounter. Fears of pregnancy or contracting venereal diseases must have an effect on your ability to experience sexual pleasure. Yet too often we do not take the time and care to protect ourselves sufficiently.

It is all too easy to say you were too caught up in the throes of passion to insert your diaphragm—until you find yourself pregnant. It might seem easier not to ask your partner if she has herpes—until you find yourself afflicted with the condition. Though it may be embarrassing to ask about sexually transmitted diseases, it is important to muster the courage. Though it may seem awkward to stop and use birth control, it may save you the stress of an unwanted pregnancy or the painful decision to have an abortion.

This week, make a commitment to your health and well-being. Protect yourself during sex. This means using birth control regularly. There are many options available for birth control, from condoms to diaphragms to spermicides to the Pill. Find the method that is best for you and use it. If you're a man, you have just as much responsibility. Ask your partner if she's using birth control; if she's not, use a condom. Most women will appreciate your thoughtfulness. A condom is also your best protection against AIDS and other sexually communicable diseases.

In addition, it is not difficult to make your use of birth control part of your sexual experience. Think of it as another kind of sharing, even a type of foreplay. For example, a woman can help a man put on a condom, and a man can help a woman insert a diaphragm or a contraceptive sponge. All of this can be done in bed, with no interruption to the excitement of the moment.

Don't forget that sexual protection also means asking questions. Don't hesitate to ask a new partner if he has had herpes or any other sexually communicable diseases. If he says yes, either postpone sex for a while or insist on using a condom.

Remember, good sex is directly connected to taking responsibility for yourself. So the next time you make love, enjoy the freedom that comes from feeling safe on all levels. Use birth control, and ask questions. It may be embarrassing, but a little discomfort now can save you a lot of pain later on.

Saying yes to sex.

☐

Do you find yourself saying no to sex too often? There are times when no is appropriate and important, but if you're not careful, that no could become a habit. You may start out with valid reasons for your refusal. You're tired; it's too late; you've got work that must be done; you're just not in the mood. Then before you turn around, a month has gone by and you've had no sex. At this point, you may find that you are so used to saying no that you don't know how to say yes anymore.

This week, say yes to sex. If your partner asks you to make love, put aside all your excuses. Trust that your work will wait. Sex might even clear your head so that you can return to your work more relaxed and efficient. If it is one A.M., just accept that you may be a little tired tomorrow. Besides, you might be surprised by how energized you'll feel in the morning after the deeply relaxing sleep that good sex can bring. If you're not in the mood, say yes anyway. You just might become turned on once you've gotten started.

But saying yes to the physical act of sex is not enough. You need to say yes to giving yourself fully to the experience. If you agree to have sex and then hold back during the encounter, it may be no better than saying no to begin with. Holding back during sex is just a silent or secret no that can turn an encounter into an unpleasant experience for you and your partner.

It may be scary to say yes to sex so completely. But the ability to become totally involved is one of the main ingredients necessary for satisfying sex. Give it a try. This week, go beyond your fear and your resistance. Try saying yes with all of you. This experiment may open you to a great deal of pleasure and fun.

I accept the ups and downs of my sexual life.

All too often, we expect sex to be a perfect experience. We believe it should lift us to ecstatic heights, and that this ecstasy should happen as a matter of course. We have been raised on the Hollywood model of passionate embraces and shooting stars. When our own sexual experience falls short of this ideal, we assume there's something wrong with us.

While sex is most certainly capable of lifting us to great heights, it is not something that happens every day. When a relationship is new and we are falling in love, sex can feel wondrous. One kiss is enough to make us weak in the knees. But if we expect sex always to be like this, we are setting ourselves up for disappointment.

The truth is that our sexual experience is as varied and intricate as we are. Sometimes sex is like fireworks, but other times, it is quiet and comfortable, maybe even awkward. Sometimes an orgasm will leave you shuddering. Other times it will be no more than a quiet quiver. Your mood, your energy level, the day-to-day fluctuations of your life, will affect your sexual life. Other times, there will not even be a direct relationship between your general mood and your desire to have sex. You may feel fantastic emotionally and yet find your sexual encounter surprisingly low-key.

Whatever you experience, it is important to accept yourself sexually. Accept the highs and lows, and the movement from one to the other. Let go of any fixed standards you may be trying to live up to. If you fixate on demanding that sex always match a certain idea, you deny the flux of life itself.

This week, when you make love, give yourself total permission to be just where you are. If you are feeling happy and fulfilled, that's great. If you are feeling quiet or shy, that's okay, too. Just know that the beauty of your sexual life is that it will change. Discover the pleasure and excitement that lies in following the currents and riding the waves. Discover the pleasure of celebrating who you are.

ABOUT THE AUTHOR

BARBARA GLABMAN-COHEN practices psychotherapy in New York City. She has an M.A. in Sexuality from New York University, where she also earned her B.S. in Education. Currently, she co-leads workshops on "What Love Can Do" with Pat Rodegast, Emmanuel, and her husband William. She is also offering workshops on homosexuality; on intimacy, sexuality, and relationships; and on the spiritual meaning of sexuality throughout the United States.

Ms. Glabman-Cohen instituted a program at the Vanderbilt Clinic of Columbia Presbyterian Hospital counseling teenagers in sexuality, birth control, and parenting.

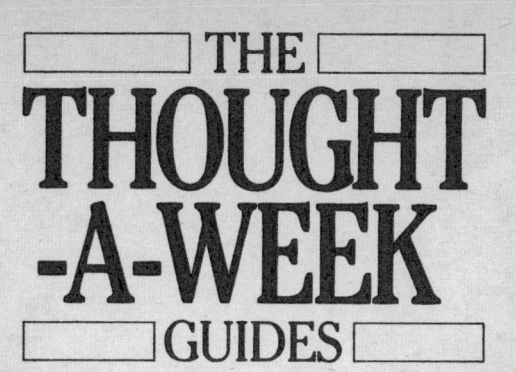

THE
THOUGHT
-A-WEEK
GUIDES

Each book contains 52 insights, one for each week of the year to help you achieve your goals effectively and efficiently. Designed to give you expert advice, each volume is written in an up-beat, informal style by a specialist in each particular field.

TA-162